to have Loved

Wendy Killian

Tate Publishing & *Enterprises*

To Have Loved

Published by Tate Publishing & Enterprises, LLC
127 E. Trade Center Terrace | Mustang, Oklahoma 73064 USA
1.888.361.9473 | www.tatepublishing.com

Tate Publishing is committed to excellence in the publishing industry. The company reflects the philosophy established by the founders, based on Psalm 68:11,
"The Lord gave the word and great was the company of those who published it."

Cover design by Amber Gulilat
Interior design by Blake Brasor

Published in the United States of America

ISBN: 978-1-60799-032-1
1. BIOGRAPHY & AUTOBIOGRAPHY / Religious
2. FAMILY & RELATIONSHIPS / Death, Grief, Bereavement
09.05.14

Dedication

I dedicate this book to Joy–a little girl who changed my life. I really miss you. I truly loved you, and I am so thankful that God placed you in my life for the short time you were here with us. God gave your parents a wonderful gift when he gave them you to love. I am so thankful that they allowed me to be part of your life. Your irresistible smile and big hugs are forever in my mind. Your death was the hardest thing I have faced in my life. It crushed me to a depth that I had never experienced before. It also stirred a hunger and a passion in me for more of Jesus in my life.

Joy, it was through your death that I found Jesus in the deepest way. The purpose God has placed on my heart is strong. I have a desire to see people set free and for people to know Jesus the way I do. I don't understand why God brought you home to be with him at the age of two, but I know what your precious life has done to mine. Though my heart will always ache for you and your family, know that your life brought a hunger for me to know Jesus in the most intimate way. Joy, I love you.

Acknowledgements

I want to thank my husband and my children for walking with me through this. I thank them for their love and patience with me. I thank my family for listening to me, my parents for encouraging me and helping me to see clearly. I thank all my friends whom God has blessed me with. Thank you for listening to me, encouraging me, and loving me. Thank you for the many smiles and hugs I receive from everyone. These little things may not seem like much, but there is healing that flows from a simple smile and a hug, and it is from God. A smile is from the heart; it says to me things will be okay and that I am loved. Hugs are God's love pouring out of someone's arms. I thank the many people who prayed for me. I thank Theresa Hitt for all the time she put into my book, editing it for me. Thank you, Jesus, for becoming my very best friend, for showing me the depth of your love. Jesus, I owe you my life; thank you for restoring me.

Table of Contents

Foreword

Wow, what a gift! This book is a treasure of encouragement promoting passion and surrender in people's lives. If you are a person overcome by loss, this book will show you the freedom in releasing your pain and relying fully on the strength and sovereignty of God.

As Wendy shares her story of this life—changing tragedy, the pages reveal a powerful God of overwhelming peace and promise. In the depth of her struggle, amidst feelings of guilt, confusion, and rejection, God refines her and draws her ever closer unto himself. He teaches her the rewards of obedience and worship, and proves himself faithful again and again. As she learns to lay down her heaviness at the feet of Jesus, Wendy comes to understand the heart of the Father. In her quietness and trust, he satisfies her soul with undeniable hope and his healing presence.

For the past twenty years, I have understood Wendy to be one of the most genuine, compassionate, and gentle—spirited women I know. Throughout her teenage years and into marriage and motherhood, faith in God always appeared to come naturally for her. Her walk with the LORD seemed easy and unwavering. Listening to Wendy over the last three years, I have witnessed the growth of an intense relationship with God, at a depth of which I have never seen before. She experiences daily communion with the LORD and knows what it means to abide in him. Her story is a glimpse of what our all—consuming God is capable of and how immeasurable his love is for his people.

To Have Loved is a beautiful testament to the awesomeness of God! Regardless of your circumstance, Wendy's words will challenge you to a new level of faith and inspire you to delve further into relationship with the one true God. As you read her testimony, you will taste and see that the LORD is good! How glorifying! How wonderful is he!

—Kim Stariha
Blaine, Minnesota

Preface

Dear Readers,

I want to share my story with you to tell you of how God helped me overcome a painful tragedy. My prayer for you is that as you read this you will find hope. I pray that this book speaks to your heart. I never expected to walk through a horrible tragedy with people I loved so deeply. I didn't think I could ever be free from carrying the guilt of that accident. Walking through this side of a tragedy was very painful, but God brought me to deeper relationship with him, and he has restored me. God is right by you, ready to help you; he longs to bring freedom to your life. I pray as you read this book, you will allow God to restore you and bring freedom to you.

—Wendy Killian

A Friendship like Family

"But as for me in my household we will serve the LORD…"

Joshua 24:15 KJV

For twenty years, I attended the same church from childhood, to marriage, to motherhood. My husband and I were both involved in our church. It was home. A pastor that we knew very well took a job at a church a few miles away from us. Week after week, my husband and I felt God tugging us to go and visit this church. We waited and waited because we were content where we were. Deep down we knew this was more than a tug, so in April 2004, we visited this church.

Something happened when we visited. For the first two weeks we sat in service, I cried. My husband and I just knew this was where God wanted us to be. Our children were so excited to be there, too. We decided to stay. We had such a joy and excitement to accept the move God put into our hearts.

When my family and I made the decision to move to a

new church, we knew we wanted to get involved and find a place to serve. My love for children led me to work in the children's ministry. I taught preschoolers on Wednesday nights, and eventually became the preschool coordinator.

As we served, we started to get to know the children's pastors, Greg and Sara. By the end of the summer, our friendship started to grow, and our kids loved being together. Greg and Sara had an excitement about them that was contagious. They had "fun" written all over them. We would talk almost every day, and would hang out at least once a week. Our friendship grew quickly, and it felt deep, like family.

One day my husband and I were talking, and we decided that it would be fun to prank them some how. We decided to "flamingo" their yard. It was funny; they never expected it to be us. When we were at church the next day, they kept asking people who did it. We didn't say anything. We decided the next day to do it again. Two more flamingos showed up in their yard. One night over dinner, my husband and I looked at each other and said, "Should we tell them?" They had a nervous look on their faces; I am sure they were wondering what we were going to tell them. When we told them we flamingoed their house, they were so surprised. Watching them trying to figure out who had done it was quite a thrill.

When Greg and Sara would go out of town, they would give us the keys to their house so we could get their mail. The first time they gave us the keys, I smiled, wondering if they realized they had given me their keys. What an opportunity! I had to take advantage of having the keys to their house. We discovered the thrill of hiding things in their house that would surprise them, like a fake mouse or bugs. One time, we even hid a small alarm clock next to their bed and set it to go off very early in the morning. We had a lot of fun; I never got tired of being with them.

A lot of times late at night, they would surprise us after our kids went to bed. They would drive up next to the window facing our driveway and knock on the window. They were night owls, but I was one who didn't normally stay up too late. Greg got us hooked on playing Game Cube, so they would come in, and we'd play Game Cube, each one trying to beat everyone else. Many nights when they came, I would already be in my pajamas, but that made it even more fun.

I really loved them and their kids, and serving became even more fun because we were working with our friends. We spent a lot of time together in church and outside of church. We had a bond only God could give. Greg and Sara had three children. I watched their kids often when they needed help. The kids loved coming over to our house, and we really loved their kids. They felt like family. Their kids even spent a week with us and our four children while Greg and Sara were at a children's pastors' conference in California. For one week, we had seven kids, aged seven months to seven years old. My husband took the week off to help me. I'd have to say it was busy, but it went very well. The night before they were to leave for California, Greg, Sara, and their kids slept at our house because they had to fly out very early in the morning. We stayed awake so long visiting that night that they only ended up with two hours of sleep.

Sometimes when I would call and talk to Sara, Joy would be fussing in the background. Sara would put the phone up to her ear and let me talk to her. Joy would stop fussing!

I loved it. Some days I'd ask Sara if I could take the two girls to my house to spend time with my kids and me. She would look at me and say, "You're crazy," because I had four of my own. But our kids loved being together, and seeing how much fun they had made it worth it.

We had just spent some time during the last five days in a row together because of the Fourth of July activities and church. On July 5th, Greg and I talked on the phone about how we felt there was something so different and deep with our families—a bond that God gave all of us. Greg and Sara were very special to me. I loved having them as friends. We had so much fun being together, It felt as if I known them my whole life. They weren't just the children's pastors. For over two years, Greg and Sara, along with their three children, also cleaned the church as a part—time job, most nights usually cleaning until midnight. My heart went out to them. I wanted to help them. Most Wednesday nights after church my husband would take our kids home and I stayed and helped them so they could get done cleaning sooner and get their kids home to bed. Many nights I would be vacuuming the church holding Joy or her baby brother in one arm and vacuuming in the other arm. There was one night after I helped them clean the church that Sara looked at me and said, "I have never had a friend like you."

On July 6, 2005, things changed forever. Greg, Sara, their kids, and I had just spent the whole day working together on projects at church. I went home for a couple of hours, then came back that evening and finished Wednesday night church. Like every other Wednesday night after church ended, it was time to clean. But this week, I decided to go home early because my husband was on vacation all week. It was about 9:30 p.m., so I loaded my four children in my full—size van, and drove up by the front doors to say goodnight to my friends. Greg brought Joy to my window to say goodbye to me, and then Greg and Joy went inside the church. Sara was at my passenger window talking to me. We finished talking and then we said goodbye to each other. My husband, who was in his car next to me on my passenger side, started to leave first. Then, about thirty seconds later, I started to leave. I only drove a few feet when I felt something with my back tire. In my mind, I thought I bumped the curb. But then I heard my friend scream horribly, and I knew something was very wrong. It was Joy. I never heard or saw her. Somehow she snuck out of the church unnoticed and walked right in front of my van. That was the worst night of my life.

Joy was a happy two—year—old girl. Her smile was so amazing that it would give my stomach butterflies. Her eyes would spark with excitement when you said her name. She gave me such big hugs and kisses when I held her in my arms. She would look at me and say with such a sweet smile, "My Wen We." I could feel Joy's love when I held her in my arms. I truly loved her. She was beautiful. She had light brown natural curls in her hair that came from her mom. Sweetness just oozed from her. Joy was a wonderful gift from God to her parents and all that knew her.

Joy asked to come to my house every week. If I invited her older sister to come over to play with my girls, Joy would insist on coming to my house too. I felt so tickled inside that she wanted to come see me. At naptime when I would baby—sit, I would hold and rock her. I would look at her with a smile and say, "Go night—night." She would smile at me, wrap her fingers in mine, close her eyes, and most times, would fall right to sleep. I thought, *Man, that was so easy; I couldn't even get my own kids to do that*. Her parents must have been so proud.

Joy was so sweet. She loved watching *The Wiggles* videos. One day I sent one home with Joy's mom, Sara, and Joy just loved it. Sara jokingly thanked me for getting her hooked on it. Joy was so creative. She could turn videotapes into purses by pulling a little of the videotape out of the case. Being sticky was fun to her. I took her swimming a few times with my children and me. She would just jump right into the water, keeping me on my toes chasing after her. She was very brave. She had no fear of water; she loved it.

Joy was a berry thief. Her parents, Greg and Sara, had a few strawberry plants in their backyard. Sometimes, we would sit outside in their backyard and visit while our kids played. Joy would find the plants and eat the strawberries off them before they could pick them.

My son, Cody, and Joy played together; they were only about five months apart in age. When he would do something wrong, he would look at me and say, "Joy did it."

Joy then would look at me and say, "Cody did it." It was so funny.

She seemed to like biting Cody from time to time. I am sure he somehow instigated it. After she would bite, she would look at me with such a sweet smile and soft voice and say, "Sorry." She was so irresistible.

One day we had Greg and Sara over for lunch with their kids. We noticed that it was awfully quiet and thought we better see what Cody and Joy were up to. We found them in the bathroom, completely soaked from their heads to their toes with toilet water. They found combs in the vanity and must have thought they should dip them into the toilet to comb their hair. They were so soaked, and we couldn't stop laughing. They were double trouble together.

Moments after the Accident

I was in shock; I was so scared. All I could think was, *Where did she come from? How could this happen?* I would never hurt Joy; I loved my friends so much. *What just happened?* I looked and pulled away. I just watched Joy being taken inside the building a few minutes before. There were no kids outside, only a few of us getting ready to go. *Where did she come from, and why didn't any of us see her?* Everything inside of me screamed, *This isn't possible; this can't be happening!* I was terrified.

I immediately got out of the van. By this time, my husband was to the end of the parking lot. He heard all the screaming and turned around to see what had happened. My four children jumped out of the van and tried to follow me. They all saw Joy, a friend that they loved and spent a lot of time with, and they were scared. I turned and looked at my kids and said, "Get back in the van." Within a few seconds my husband was with them and put them in his car. I asked him to take them home. They were all quiet and scared.

Right after the accident, Sara and I knelt beside Joy to see if she was okay. Sara checked for a heartbeat but there was none. Greg ran in the church and called 911. With the weight of the van, Joy died instantly. I started pacing and praying for God to touch her.

Right away Sara stood up for a moment and wrapped her arms around me and said, "I love you, and I forgive you," over and over. Then she walked over to the grass and started pounding on the ground crying. Greg walked around in complete shock with his hands on his head in terror. I kept telling them, "I am so sorry. I am sorry. I never saw her." A friend of Sara's pulled her aside and held her while a neighbor to the church ran over and pulled me aside and sat with me and held me until the police came. Once the police came, we were separated, and I had to sit in the police car for the next hour or so. I felt so scared and alone. I was shaking. I didn't think Greg and Sara knew where I was. I thought they thought I went home. I kept telling the police, "Greg and Sara don't know where I am. Can I go in the church and see them?" but the police kept saying no; they needed to take our statements. As the different pastors that worked at the church arrived and came to talk to me, I kept sending them into the church to tell my friends that I was stuck in the police car. I wanted to be with them; I needed to be with them. I couldn't stand it. I felt so alienated, like I was abandoning them in the hardest moment of their life. I couldn't do anything but sit in the police car and wait. All I could think about was how I was going to be hated by everyone. As I was sitting in the police car all alone, I told God, "I know I am going to hate walking through this, but I promise I will not turn from you.

While I sat in the police car, someone brought me a note from Sara that she wrote inside the church. The note read:

> Wendy, my sister in the cities, I love you. I don't blame you. I forgive you. I know it was an accident, and I am sorry any of this is happening.

Sara and I were like sisters, we could talk about anything, and I really loved her. I hung on to that note and read it over and over for many days.

I had to leave with the police to go to the hospital for a blood test. I remember as we started to leave the parking lot, looking out the window and the TV news crew was sitting there. That was the last thing I wanted to see; I so badly just wanted to hide. During the next couple of days, the newspapers kept trying to call and talk to me, but I wouldn't answer; I couldn't. My house was flooded with people trying to console me and remind me that they loved me. I was told to give Sara and Greg time, but I needed to talk to them. After a couple of days I called them sobbing, apologizing, pleading for them to forgive me. Sara's mom answered the phone and talked to me with so much love and said no one blamed me.

Before the funeral, I asked our pastor if I could talk to Greg and Sara. I needed to see them. He talked to them and they agreed to come over to my house. I wrote them a letter pouring out my heart to them. I had my pastor read it out loud. This is an excerpt from my letter:

> July 9th
> Greg and Sara, two of my best friends, I love you with such a deep love. My heart is so torn apart inside. Joy meant a lot to me; I loved her as if she was my own. I don't understand… I just can't understand. *Why me? Why you?* I ask God continually, "Why… why… why?" It is not fair. You know my heart and how I would do anything for you both.
>
> I don't want to lose you. I really love you both. I love your children with all my heart. I am so very sorry. I hope you can forgive me. I know it was an accident, but I need your forgiveness.
>
> I loved Joy so much; she was my little buddy. Please know my heart. This is the worst thing I have ever faced. I just want to hide, but people won't leave me alone. I feel horrible. I feel like I am on the wrong side. I want to be with you guys, holding you. It's not fair. I don't understand why God didn't do something; I can't understand. I don't want to live with this; it is tearing me up inside…

When Greg and Sara came over to our house to talk with us, they did something that surprised me. They brought me flowers. It had ten white daisies that represented our two families and one pink rose in the middle representing Joy. It made me cry. My heart broke with thoughts of Joy. Sara also wrote me an amazing letter that read:

July 9th

Wendy and Tom,

God woke me up at four o'clock a.m. this morning. My heart was aching for you. You guys mean so much to us. I know God was the one who brought us together in the first place. I will not let Satan tear us apart. We were more than friends; we were family. We celebrated together and cried together.

Wendy, you are an amazing friend. I have never met anyone like you. You are caring and selfless. I have learned so much from you guys, things you probably don't even know.

I don't understand why everything happened the way they did. You were Joy's second family. I can hear her say, "My Wen We and my Tom." She had such love and trust in you like she had for no one else. This is going to be the hardest thing we will ever have to go through.

There is so much pain, but once again this is when our friendship comes into play. Let's join together and walk through this valley together. It's dark and painful. But Joy is a shining light. She loved life and lived it to the fullest, and now what a better place could she be but sitting in Jesus's arms?

Let's surround her light and let it drown out all the guilt and pain and sorrow. Let's celebrate the memory of her life—all the things she did to make us smile, all the funny faces she made, all the bite marks Cody has. Let's remember the beauty and happiness she brought us.

> I don't know why we didn't get to keep her longer, but I am glad we got to share her with you. God is holding her now, and she is beautiful. Let God hold us now too. Let his love surround us, and let us show his beauty also. Let us remember her in her life. Tom and Wendy, we love you.
>
> Greg and Sara

When we were at the funeral, my head was down. I felt as low as I could feel. Then Sara came up to me, gave me a big hug, and looked at me with such love. She said to me, "When I look at you, all I am thinking about is that you're my best friend." I didn't feel worthy of Sara wanting me as a friend, and I started crying even more.

They invited me to the burial site with the rest of the family after the funeral. As the pastor was talking, I stood there with my head down weeping, desperately wanting to turn back time. I wanted Joy here with us. As I was crying, Sara walked up to me and handed me a rose that represented Joy. I was honored, but in brokeness I wanted to fall to the ground. I knew Joy's death was a total accident, but I felt like it was all my fault that Joy wasn't here. My head was just spinning.

I have never been so broken and crushed in my life. This was such a horrible nightmare that just kept replaying itself over and over in my mind. I just wanted to die. How was I going to handle this? How could I watch my friends hurt so deeply? How could I not carry the guilt of Joy's death? How could I bear this tremendous load that was upon me? My heart felt like it was ripped wide open.

I questioned God and asked him over and over,

"Why...why...why would you allow this to happen? Why didn't you stop it from happening? I just don't understand...Why my closest friends' child? Why not me or my child? God, you know what Joy meant to me; you know how much I loved my friends...God, why?" I couldn't understand, and it didn't make any sense to me at all. Every part of my mind was screaming. I was so mad at God for allowing this to happen. I would question him over and over, "God, what did I do to deserve this? All I ever tried to do was love my friends and their kids and serve you, and this is what I get? You allowed me to be the one in the driver's seat? You knew she was there. You could have stopped it; why didn't you? God!"

I was so broken, and I just sobbed day after day. How could I possibly live through this? How could I carry this nightmare? If only I had not driven up to the front doors to say goodnight to my friends. Joy would still be here if I hadn't been driving. Why would God allow me to be in this horrid place? I was filled with "what if's" and "if only's." My friends' child was gone, and they were hurting deeply, far beyond words can describe. How could I handle this? What would I do? This couldn't be happening! I did not want to live through this. I really wanted to die so I wouldn't have to bear what was happening. But I had to somehow make it. I still had four young children and a husband who needed me.

Every single day for months, before I got out of bed, my heart pounded, I continually felt like Joy was gone because of me and that I hurt my friends more than words could describe. My mind was bombarded, thinking everyone was must be looking down on me, blaming me. I felt like a complete failure. I would tell God, "I don't think I can bear this today… this is too heavy. God, make it stop, please make it go away." I was in such a dark heavy place. And every morning for months, before I got out of bed, God would continue to whisper, "Just trust me. I will not let you down." I would ask God day after day, "Are you sure I can handle this LORD? Because I don't think I can; this is too heavy. I can't live with this." Somehow, he helped me and gave me hope.

Little did I know how real God would become to me in the next year as I dealt with the horror of the accident. I had no idea of the things God would teach me or how he would bring me to stand and live again in freedom.

Worship

"The Lord thy God in the midst of thee is mighty..."
Zephaniah 3:17 KJV

I loved my friends very much. My heart ached to know how much they were hurting over the loss of their daughter. It felt like a nail was being driven into my heart continually. I truly loved Joy; she was so special to me. Even though it was a total accident, I was carrying the guilt of her death. I was so broken. I really wanted to be the one to comfort and love on my friends and carry them through this. I was told I needed to give them time. Not being able to comfort my friends broke my heart. My arms literally ached every day to hold them. I didn't want them to hurt. If I could take it all away from them, I would. But I was such a mess myself and somehow I needed to try to get stronger so I could be there for my friends.

I never wanted so badly to die until this point. Life had always seemed smooth for me. There was nothing too horrible that would make me want to give up. But this was so horrible—a child I loved was gone and my friends were hurting deeply. My mind was hit hard. Besides grieving for Joy, I found that I was facing the biggest battle I ever faced in my mind.

People everywhere were so amazing to me; they poured such love on me. My phone wouldn't stop ringing, and for weeks, I would sometimes receive thirty calls a day. I was flooded with over a hundred cards. No one ever had a negative word or any blame; people continually poured love and encouragement over me. So many people would look at me and say, "If this could happen to you, it could happen to us." They carried the burden with me, easily putting themselves in my place.

So much love was poured on me, and that was very healing to me. But that didn't stop my thoughts. Every day after I woke up and before I would get out of bed, Satan would put a new convincing lie in my mind, like, "Today is the day everyone will hate you," or, "Look at how much you hurt your friends." The thoughts were so real that it felt as if I was sinking, and the heaviness took over me. I felt even more depressed. It was really hard to think clearly past those thoughts.

It had been a couple weeks since the accident, and I hadn't looked to God like I normally did. I had so many people reassuring me that it was an accident, trying to help me get past it. Of course, I knew it was an accident and that there was nothing I could've done. I could hear them speak truth to me, but my mind couldn't grasp it. I was a mess inside, carrying the guilt of that accident.

A couple weeks after the accident, a friend stopped at my house. God put on his heart that day to tell me that when the enemy is hitting your mind, to get on your knees and worship. I said okay. I loved to pray, but very rarely did I kneel, so this was new for me. The next day my mind was hit hard with thoughts like, "I know that my friends just hate me." Even though this wasn't true, my fears consumed me, and I was having a hard time clearing my head. I had so much anxiety over my thoughts that it hurt to even breathe; the heaviness was too much. I didn't know how to clear my thoughts. I decided to put some worship music on. I got down on my knees before God, crying and asking him to help me, and I started to worship him.

Something happened when I did that. As I knelt and worshiped, God whispered to me, "Don't worry. I am in control, and I will take care of you. Just let go and trust me." At that moment, I thought to myself, *There is no way I can fix this; there is absolutely nothing I can do.* So I surrendered every thought and feeling I was dealing with, and handed it to Jesus. The heaviness at that moment lifted, and I felt his peace begin to flood over me. I began to think clearly. I had hope.

Worship is something so powerful. God created us to worship him. It is something that our soul longs for. Only God can truly satisfy us completely. Why did I have to worship when I felt so depressed? Well, worship takes us somewhere. It takes us right into God's presence. Worship takes the focus off of us and our problems and puts the focus on God. Once we can look past ourselves, and look to him, it allows God to move. It allows him to pour out his peace on us. He cannot help us if we are trying to be in control.

When you truly worship God, you surrender your ways to his ways. He then begins to fill your heart with himself.

When you worship God, you open the door to enter into his presence. It doesn't matter where you are, if you can just worship and cry out to him, he will come in and begin to fill you with his peace. His presence is amazing; nothing can compare to being with God.

It's hard to take the time for worship or even to make an effort, especially when your heart is breaking and you can't stop the tears from flowing. Where do you find strength to worship God when the depression you feel brings you exhaustion and the heaviness you carry weighs you down? How can you worship when you feel like there is no hope?

At times, it is a sacrifice. But a sacrifice that is well worth it. You are trading your sorrows for his joy, his peace. When you're so far down you think nothing can ever lift you back up again, that is the furthest thing from the truth. God is always by your side, for you are never alone. The moment you cry out and worship him, his presence will begin to fill you with his peace and he will give you hope. Even though I know how much it will help me, there are days that I struggle to take that time with God. There were many days when I was so depressed and I just didn't feel like it, it took everything I had to look past myself and the mess I was in to worship him. I learned something: God honors sacrifice. He sees the sacrifice it is for us. He knows how it sometimes takes everything you have to look up to him, and it truly pleases him that you still do.

God absolutely loves to spend time with us. He longs so deeply to be with us. He waits for us to spend time with him. Just as much as we desire to be filled by God, he desires to fill us. He wants to fill us with his peace. He waits for us to reach out to him. God loves us so much more than we can imagine, and he desires for us to love him, really love him.

I thought to myself, *Why do I have to get on my knees and worship when the enemy is hitting my mind? Why was it so important to God to send someone to tell me that? Why on my knees?* Kneeling before God is a sign of surrender to God, and Satan hates that. Satan has no choice. It is his worst fear that we run to God. Psalms 22:3 NIV says, "God inhabits our praises." As we praise and worship, God enters in. As I went before God, Satan had to flee. He is not welcome in God's presence, and as we draw near to God, Satan is ordered to flee.

Kneeling before God every day is where I started to find strength. Each day, over and over for so many months, I would hear the thoughts the enemy pounded my mind with. I would cry, and a heaviness would come over me. I felt like giving up. How do you ever get past carrying the guilt even though it was totally an accident? How?

Well, each time the negative thoughts filled my mind, I began to worship and get down on my knees before God. It didn't matter where I was, even if I was in the bathroom and my mind was spinning, I would get down right there and cry out, "God, help me, please!" God would set my mind free. He would fill me with his truth. Even though I would seek him and feel freed in my mind, later that same day, over and over, the enemy would continue to fill my mind with negative, accusing thoughts. Many days, I had to go before God and worship him at least three times a day so he could continue to set my mind free, fill me again with his peace and hope, and carry my heavy burden.

Second Corinthians 12:9–10 NIV says, "God's strength

is made perfect in our weakness. When we are weak he is strong." I thought about that. *Your strength is made perfect in my weakness, when I am weak you are strong. How can that be? What is it about me being so weak that causes you to be so strong?* When we run out of our strength and we cry out to God to help us, it enables his miraculous power to invade us and give us his strength. His strength is then made perfect in our weakness. Whatever you're facing, no matter how low you feel, as you seek God and cry out to him, something will happen. His strength will fill you, helping you face another day. The more time you can spend with God, the stronger you will become. His strength is amazing and it never runs out. But we need to seek him and worship him so he can fill us and give us strength. "The LORD is my strength and my shield; my heart trusts in him and I am helped" (Psalms 28:7 NIV).

God and I have an agreement. At times, I wanted to carry it. I didn't feel like taking the time out to give it to God. It was work to truly hand it over to him. But over time, I got to a point that I said to God, "What else is there for me to do but release what is on my heart and on my mind to you?" I could think about it, consume myself with it, and try to make it work. But if I could surrender to God—Joy's death, my racing thoughts—he would carry my worries, and I could be free. What an awesome deal. So I surrendered my burden to him, laid it at his feet, and at that moment, he would lift that heaviness.Psalms 55:22 NIV says, "Cast all your cares on the LORD for he will sustain you, he will not let the righteous fall." What an awesome promise God has given us. Think about that: If we give him our cares and worries, he *will* sustain us. Just the thought of that promise makes me excited. God gave me a tremendous amount of peace when I spent time with him. I received an incredible amount of peace through worship, reading, or being still in his presence. It was "A peace that passes all understanding" (Philippians 4:7 NIV).

My surrendering to him was me on my knees before God, telling him that I can't do this on my own and that I needed him every moment of the day. I thought to myself, *I surrendered all my heartaches and longings to God already today; that should be enough.* But it wasn't. It was a daily surrender—many times hourly surrender—crying to him until I couldn't cry anymore, telling him that I needed his help and that I could not make it through this on my own. I needed him desperately! Worship is surrendering to God. Even after God taught me this, I still had days where I was pounded in my mind and days that were hard. But now at least, I was learning how to fight the battle in my mind.

At times I would walk in to church, and people would look at me that knew me, see me smiling, and say, "Wow, you look like you're doing good." But they didn't know what it took for me to have that smile, to have that peace. It took giving what I was carrying to God, crying out to him, giving my heartaches to him, and worshiping him throughout my day, over and over. Then the next day, I was waking up, facing the oppressive thoughts in my mind. I was beginning with the same process again, crying out to God to give me that peace, to carry my burden. And you know, each day he has always been and will always be faithful to give his strength and peace. It is so worth it! He *will* sustain you.

Now, a couple of years later, I still face days that, when

the memory of everything floods me, I just want to give up and scream and just run away from it all. In those moments that I feel overwhelmed, I try my hardest to look to God, worship him, and hand the accident back to him again. I try my hardest to seek him. He then fills me fresh again with his peace, and I have hope to make it through another hour, another day.

God showed me it doesn't matter what you go through in life. When you are in his presence, alone with God, truly worshiping him and spending time with him, you will notice nothing else really matters because you are with your creator. When you are worshiping God, it is all about him.

What are you facing that weighs you down, that feels way too heavy to carry? Have you, like me, had an accident that was out of your control, that you are carrying the guilt for? Is it your thoughts or something that happened to you or someone close to you? No matter what you're facing today, God is big enough to pull you up and give you his peace and hope. If you can get alone with him, even for a few minutes, and worship him and release to him what is heavy on your heart, he will begin to fill you with his peace. He will give you strength and healing. He is right by your side waiting for you to reach out and call his name. He is right beside you, waiting to help you. God is so powerful. As you give him whatever burdens you bear, he will carry them and give you his peace. Continue to seek him and release it to him so you can be free.

My Best Friend

"... but there is a friend who sticks closer than a brother."
Proverb 18:24 NIV

Family and friends were always there for me to talk to and that was very healing, but I still felt alone. I talked to a pastor that walked through the same experience, and he helped me. But day in and day out, I still felt alone with my heart aching. Who would understand what I was feeling? Who could relate to the feelings I felt inside? I really needed someone who had been where I was to understand what I was battling inside of me, someone that I could really let it out to.

One afternoon, a month or so after the accident, I was driving, and God reminded me, "Remember I am the Wonderful Counselor" (Isaiah 9:6 NIV). I was taken aback, surprised, yet in awe that he would remind me of that part of his title, of who he is. I thought to myself, *Oh yeah, you're right. You do have that title, and if I want someone to be there for me, day in and day out to help me, you would be the best one.* Jesus would be the one I unloaded every feeling I felt to, I would let him be my Wonderful Counselor. If he was going to remind me that he is the Wonderful Counselor, then I expected him to help me. Little did I realize how much I would come to know about my God.

Every day I'd cry. I didn't feel like calling anyone and crying to them, because for so many months it was the same thing I was feeling over and over, and I didn't think anyone would really understand. So I would just sit on my floor in my bedroom crying to God and unloading what was on my heart. I would tell him exactly how I was feeling inside at those moments. After I poured out my thoughts and feelings, I started to feel freedom. I felt his peace come in and calm me; I started to have hope. I could even feel the joy that only he can give. I have never felt so close to God in my life; it was intimate. He is the one who I poured out my heart to each day. Right in the middle of my hardest days, I experienced such a sweet presence of God.

Psalms 62:8 NIV says, "Trust him at all times . . . pour out your hearts to him, for he is our refuge." God never gets tired of hearing what is on our mind or hearing us cry out in our pain. He already knows what we feel, but he wants to hear it. He wants us to talk to him like we would our closest friend. He wants to hear what is truly on our heart. He's not looking for you to use big words to talk to him; he just wants us to be completely real with him. God is waiting there for you to reach out and grab hold of him; he wants to help.In John 14, it talks about how Jesus sent the Holy Spirit to us to be our comforter, to be our counselor. I could hear when God would speak something to my heart before, but something happened when I unloaded what was on my heart each day to him, something cool. After I would cry out to him and worship him, I would sit still before him in the quietness of my room. Sometimes in the quietness, it seemed he would share his heart with me. At times, as I would share my pain with God, he would share what causes his heart to ache also. God understood what I was feeling, for in so many ways, though we may not realize it, his heart aches deeply.

One day God told me, *I know your heart, and I see it. You need to let it all go, and just trust me. Love me more than anything, and it shall be given unto you because I know what is best for* you. In Psalms 139:1 NIV, the psalmist writes, "O LORD you have searched me and know me." In the same way, he knew my heart. It just amazed me when I grasped that. It doesn't matter what others may think; God looks on the inside and sees the attitudes and motives in our heart. He knows what is inside of you. Even if everything around you is turned upside down and you feel like you can't see clearly who you are anymore, God still does. He knows what is inside you, and in reality, that is what truly matters. God sees your heart.

When I was angry with God, I questioned why he allowed this to happen. I told him all I wanted to do was just pour out my love on my friends, and this is what he allowed to happen. I felt like everything I did to show my love to them was shattered because of this horrible accident. He then led me to a verse in my Bible: "God is not unjust; he will not forget your work and the love you have shown as you helped his people and continue to help them" (Hebrews 6:10 NIV). All I could think was, *God, you did not forget my heart; you saw how much I loved them. You know, and that is what really matters.* It really gave me peace when I understood that he sees our heart.

How do we make God our closest friend? How does that happen? How do you grow a close friendship with a friend? You spend time with them. You talk to them. You're real and intimate, you listen, and you trust them. That is how it is with God. He wants to be your closest friend. He wants you to be intimate; he wants to hear what is on your heart. You may think, *But he already knows, why do I have to tell him?* Because he wants that fellowship with you. He loves to spend time with you. He wants to hear what you have to say. He wants you. He never gets tired of hearing you cry out to him with your hurts or telling him your joys. He also wants you to listen to him. I always talked to God. But now when I talk to him, I talk to him like he is sitting right beside me. I tell him exactly what is on my mind.

While listening to a song by Jeff Deyo, I heard something that forever changed the way I thought. This is what I heard: "God's desires for us will truly bring us the true happiness, give us the most peace and joy. God's desires will satisfy our souls deeply. We just really need to trust him and to be satisfied in God and God alone."

That was something that forever changed my thoughts. From that point on, I really wanted to know what God's desires for me are. I knew what would make me happy. I thought what would make me the happiest is for everything to go back to the way it was. I wanted my friendship with Greg and Sara to continue to grow and to be able to walk through this with them, by their side. But if God truly, ultimately knew what would make me the happiest, that is what

I wanted more than anything. I wanted his desires for me, whatever that was. I was now looking for what God's desires would be; I was about to surrender all my desires for his.

Obedience

"If you love me, you'll obey what I command."
John 14:15 NIV

I wanted what God wanted for me so badly. I kept thinking about how important it was for him to tell me to love him more than anything, and that if I did, he would do what is best for me. I wanted to know what that was, so that was my next step, to "*love him with all my heart*" (Deuteronomy 6:5 NIV).

It had been almost two months after the accident, and I wondered why God would keep telling me over and over to just trust him and let go of my friends. In my mind that did not make any sense at all. *Let go of them, no way!* How could I when I loved them so much and when they were walking through the worst time in their lives? How could I just give them over to God and sit back and wait? It didn't make any sense to me.

More than anything, I wanted to be there for them, to comfort them. Even for me to see them hurt so deeply would cause my heart to ache. I still wanted to be there for them, even if it hurt. I would try my hardest when I was with them to be strong for them. I cared about them so much and wanted to be by their side. I told God, "They will think I don't care if I pull back and hand them to you." God knew how badly I wanted to be there for them.

Has God ever asked you to give up something and lay it down, something so dear to your heart, not knowing if he'll ever give it back to you? This family meant so much to me; to give them back to God caused my heart to ache.

I argued with God about it for almost two months. Why would God put them in my life, give them to me to love, and then ask me to give them back to him in the worst time of our lives? It didn't make sense to me. I couldn't just let go; I needed to be there for them. Then one day God said to me, "I know how much you love them; do you love them enough to give them back to me?"

I started to think about what it means to truly obey what God asked of me. I really wanted to know why he was asking me this. I still talked to them and worked together with them at church, but outside of church, I had to give them to God. Even when I would try to call Sara and Greg after the second month, they didn't answer any of my calls. Before the accident, we talked just about every day and spent a lot of time together. They were my closest friends. And now, the only time we spoke was at church. It was one of the hardest things for me to do. I didn't just do it once and say, "I obeyed God, I let go." No, it was daily letting go, surrendering them to God for over a year and a half with tears; it felt as if I was grieving over them too.

I wanted to obey what God asked me to do. So I got out

my Bible and books and was on a search to see what it meant to be obedient to God. I was reading in the *Purpose Driven Life,* and it talked about obeying God. As I read, I soaked in what it said. God doesn't owe you a reason for everything he asks you to do. Understanding can wait, but obedience can't. I wanted to understand what he asked of me now, and then I would obey, but that isn't what God wanted me to do. He wanted my obedience first. I also read that instant obedience can teach you more about God than a lifetime of Bible discussions. That really spoke to me. Then I read that you'll never understand some of God's commands until you obey them first. "Obedience unlocks understanding." It was telling me that as I continue to obey God, he will bring the understanding.

As I was searching on what it meant to truly be obedient to God, I came across this verse: "The LORD your God is testing you to find out whether you love him with all your heart and with all your soul" (Deuteronomy13:3 NIV). Obedience to God proves we really love him enough to do what he asks of us.

"Okay," I told God, "I will try my hardest. If this is what you want me to do, I will obey." I had to surrender Greg and Sara to God day after day on my knees. The longing in my heart for my friends was so strong that it just ached and I just cried. To me it felt like I was not only grieving over Joy but also over my friends. I loved them so much. I continued to give them back to God every day even though it hurt. I found that as I continued to surrender them to him, over time he began to give me peace. He began to fill that empty spot in my heart with himself.

God wanted to be the one I longed for; he wanted to be

my closest friend. God became my best friend. I always loved and served God my whole life, but something was different all of a sudden. Having to go before him each day and seek him and pour out my heart to him brought me such a closeness with God. I truly felt like I fell in love with Jesus. When the load I was carrying was very heavy, he was always there to pour out his love and calm me. He was there to listen to me. I now loved him in a way that was deeper. I couldn't wait each day to get alone with him, sit and talk to him, and to love on him. He now was the one I desired. I loved him more than anything. I was in a place where I loved him so much, that if I only had God and no one else, that was enough. He was enough.God wanted that place in my heart. He wanted to be first, above all. I was so busy serving him and trying to please others, he wasn't truly number one. But now, in the quietness he brought me to, he was. I wouldn't give God up for anything. God never got tired of hearing me cry on his shoulder, the same thing, day after day. He didn't get tired of me complaining to him about how I felt. He was always there to listen to me. Even though I still struggled with everything in my mind about the accident, he was always there to remind me of his promises, that he will never leave me and that he loved me. I realized that no matter what was going on around me, he truly loved me and he would never leave me. That was so huge to me! As much as I felt alone with the feelings I battled inside, I wasn't. Knowing God was walking with me through all this caused me to love him even more.

One day, I was going for a walk and it had been a couple months from the time I was able to let go the best I could.

God said something to me that surprised me. He asked me, "Do you want to know why I had you let go of your friends right now?"

I said, "Yes, I do." In my mind, I thought he wanted me to let go of my friends somehow for their benefit, but that was not it. He told me that he had me let go of them so he could work in me. Be my main focus and the love of my life. He wanted me to draw my strength from him and him alone. I did not realize that is why he asked me to let go of them. I thought about that, and the first couple months after the accident, when I would talk to my friends and they seemed okay with me, that gave me so much strength. But God wanted me to learn to draw my strength in a different way; he wanted me to draw it from him and him alone.

I think letting go of something or someone can be one of the hardest things to do. We worry and think, *What will happen if I do give God what he has asked? What if, after I surrender to him, he doesn't give it back to me?* It's hard to let go of someone or something and just give it to him. To release it and let God be in control. At times, we don't really trust God like we should. We try to fix it every way we can.

But God knows what is best, better than we do. I would be reminded by that quote, God's desires for us will truly make us the happiest, give us the most peace and joy. I had to remind myself that what God wanted for me would be the best thing, whatever that was. By letting it go to God and giving him control, it enables him to do his work in us without anything in his way. It is hard—taking the step of faith to let go, you may have the fear of losing someone or something and that nothing will happen. But the best possible thing can happen. If you tuck in close to God, he will fill that empty place that you surrendered to him. He will be the one you desire and love; that is what Jesus wants. He wants us to love him with all our heart, with everything. And when you get to that place, there is a peace and an inexpressible joy that comes with it.

I remembered later what I read about obedience. Obedience unlocks understanding. That started to make sense, even though when he asked me to give him my friends, I didn't understand why. But as I yielded to his ways, over time I began to understand more and more, he wanted me to totally look to him to pull me through all of this. As we obey what God asks of us and we trust him, he will bring the understanding. But what he wants is for us to trust his ways and to totally rely on him. He wants us to have faith in him.

In a book I read titled *Why,* Ann Graham Lotz wrote this: "Jesus stands ready to help us, but his help is contingent on our absolute, total obedience to His Word, whether or not we agree with it or understand it. His help is delayed and His power is bound and His glory is hidden as long as we stand around in disobedience and argue."

I wanted his help, for he knows what is best for me. Obedience is important to God. Jesus says, "If you love me you'll obey my commands" (John 14:15 NIV). God wants us to obey him; it proves we really trust him and love him. There is a freedom that comes with obeying what God asks us to do.

Is there something that you feel God has placed on your heart that he wants you to surrender to him? You may be fighting it, not understanding why he's asking you to let it go and hand it to him. But God ultimately knows what is best. He sees the bigger picture that we cannot possibly see. As you obey what God asks of you, he will show himself faithful to you, you just need to trust him and obey. God showed me that each act of obedience to him, whether big or small, allows him to trust us even more. When we are obedient to what God asks of us, he will protect us because we are obeying him.

Patience and Trust

> "*Trust in* Lord *with* all *your heart and lean not on your own understanding. In* all *your ways acknowledge him and he* will *make your paths straight.*"
>
> *Proverbs 3:4–5* NIV

I needed to learn more about being patient and waiting on God. I didn't know how long I would have to give my friends to God during this tragedy. I hoped it wouldn't be too long and that God would give them right back to me, because I just ached to comfort them and have that closeness with them. I did not know his timing in all this; all I knew was that I needed to obey what he asked me to do even though it was very hard.

As I was waiting on God, he started to teach me the importance of patience. Why do we need to be patient? Why is it so important to God? I read something cool. Faith opens the door for God to move, but patience keeps it open. I thought about that for a while, and it made a lot a sense. We can believe and have faith that God will do something; we can trust him, but if we are not willing to wait patiently on his timing, we're missing something big God wants us to learn.

A book that really helped me was the *Battlefield of the Mind* by Joyce Meyers. A friend gave it to me a year before the accident, and I never really read much of it. I found it one day and opened it up to the middle of the book. I opened it up to part three, "The Wilderness Mentalities." It taught me so much; it was like food for my soul. God started to show me a lot about the way I was thinking and more on the importance of being patient unto God. Here is what I learned: Patience is not the ability to wait, but to keep a good attitude while waiting. When we are waiting on God, we don't know how long we will have to wait for him to fulfill his plan. We think it should be now. But that isn't normally the case. God wants us to trust him and wait for him to move. Patience is very important to the LORD. He wants his children to see his character through us. Patience is powerful. It is one of the most outstanding things of God. He is so patient. "He is the same yesterday, today and forever" (Hebrews 13:8 NIV).

The method God will use to bring out patience in us is through various trials. "The testing of your faith produces patience" (James 1:3 NIV). When life is smooth and everything is going great, how much do we need to really just trust God? It's when things are shaken up that we all of a sudden start crying out, help! All of a sudden, we need to trust God to come through on our behalf for whatever the need may be.

We can't trust God and be impatient at the same time. It you think about that, it's true. In order to show God that we really trust and believe him, we need to be willing to patiently wait on him for his timing. While you're waiting on God, don't have a bad attitude. Decide to surrender it to him. Keep a good attitude, because that is what God wants to see. How you handle your problems shows your character, and your character is what you will take with you to eternity. How you choose to handle it is what matters.

I thought I had always trusted God, but I realized that at times I doubted, and wondered if he'd come through and fulfill his promises. One day, as I was unloading what was on my heart to God, he ran this verse across my mind: "Trust in the LORD with all your heart. Lean not on your own understanding. In all your ways acknowledge him and he will make your paths straight" (Proverbs 3:4–5 NIV). I always knew that verse, but the day God reminded me of it, that verse all of a sudden became alive to me. God was saying to me, "Trust me with everything. Do not even try to understand. But in everything you do acknowledge me and I will direct your steps." I didn't understand at all why everything was happening. Even now, I still don't understand why. But when God showed me that verse, he showed me that I didn't need to understand. I needed to just trust him, to keep him first and he would help me.

A few weeks after the accident, on a morning that I felt like giving up, God sent a friend to me. I didn't want to have to live through this, and I didn't want to continuously have to bear what happened. She stopped over to share with me that God told her that he knew he could trust me. I thought, *Wow, God can trust me? Why would he tell her that?* I was humbled and continued to think about that from time to time for the next month.

One day, I started to think more about that, and I told God, "If you can trust me, a human who can fail you, then why wouldn't I trust you, for you are perfect?" I told God with boldness, "If the Bible is really true and all those promises you have given us in the Bible are true, I am going to stand on those promises like never before. I am going to hold you to them until I see you fulfill them, even if it takes years. I am going to start saying them every day, reminding you of what your word says." I was going to see him be faithful.

Starting with, "For he who began a good work in you will be faithful to complete it in you" (Philippians 1:6 NIV). Then on to, "For I know the plans I have for you, plans to prosper you and not harm you, to give you a future and a hope" (Jeremiah 29:11 NIV). "For those who hope in you will not be disappointed" (Isaiah 49:23 NIV). "Because he loves me, I will rescue him. I will protect him, for he acknowledges my name. He will call upon me and I will answer. I will deliver him and honor him" (Psalm 91:14 NIV).

I found so many, many promises in the Bible that it made me so excited. I was determined to fully believe what God has promised, and see that he is true to his promises. There was a freedom inside of me when I decided I was going to really trust God, believe in his Word, and firmly stand on it. I found freedom when I decided to find hope, to understand that God knows what is best for each of our lives. "I am the LORD your God who teaches you what is best for you, who directs you in the way you should go. If only you had paid attention to my commands, your peace would be like a river…" (Isaiah 48:18–19 NIV). God can be trusted! I was determined, even if it took years, to watch him be faithful to his word. I was *expecting* to see his faithfulness.

It is not always easy to walk by faith and to trust God, to trust the unseen. To walk by faith and to trust God, it takes strength. This world we live in can be very negative and can pull you down. But go against the flow, stay strong, and believe God. He will be faithful to you. It's a promise! God loves that we trust him and that we believe he will do what is best for us. It enables him to do his work when you believe, really believe he can.

You need to trust that God knows what he is doing in your life. Many times, I still question him on everything, but what I can rest in is that he knows the future. He knows what tomorrow brings. He will be faithful in his timing. During the waiting time, allow God to teach you the things of God. Let him teach you to be patient, to trust, to love, to forgive, and so on, for that is part of what he desires to produce in us. God could answer right away, but at times, that is what the waiting time is for—to strengthen your faith and walk with him. He wants to develop your faith and trust in him even more. Life for you will be more peaceful if you can really put your trust in God. When you doubt what God can do, it hinders his hand—it keeps him from moving. You need to believe that he is true to his promises. "He will never fail you…" (Hebrews 13:5 NIV).

Giving It to God

"To you, O LORD *I lift up my soul, in you I trust, O my God."*

Psalm 25:1–2 NIV

Every single day I kept trying to figure out where Joy came from and how it all happened. I didn't know until almost two months after the accident, after the report came from the police, how the accident really happened. The police investigators found out that she was right in front of my full—size van, very close to the bumper. They said that, due to her size, I would never have seen or felt her.

One day, about six months after the accident while I was still struggling with how it happened, the morning national news did a story on the same kind of accident with a different family. They told of how, with large vehicles, there is a six— to nine—foot blind spot in front of the vehicle for a two—year—old child. They even stated that, with a full—size truck, you could put ten two—year—olds right in front of the vehicle and still not see them. I was amazed that this story was shown. God knew I needed to see that story; it helped me. I still struggled, but at least now I could understand more.

I felt I was getting stronger. I still battled thoughts, and my heart still really ached, but as I continued to surrender my thoughts to God, he was helping me. A couple of weeks after the accident, I had talked to my friends and told them I was okay with them making a claim on my van's insurance for the accident, as long as it was in truth. In my mind, I figured that is what I have insurance for, and if there is something there for them to have, I want them to have it.

If I had a million dollars, I would've wanted to give it to my friends. I loved my friends. It wouldn't bring their daughter back, but I was so sorry for what happened, I wanted to do something.

My insurance company met with me and told me they were going to deny the claim because the police investigation report stated that there was nothing that I could've done to prevent it—that it was a completely unavoidable accident. If the report would've stated I did something careless or wrong, my insurance company said they would've given the money right away. I asked my insurance company every which way to try to make it work for my friends, but the answer was no.

I left sad that day. As I walked out of the building, I looked up to God and said, "If it is according to your will, you can make this happen; you can do anything." It was my desire for my friends to have this money more than anyone, but it was totally out of my hands. There was nothing I could do. I knew I had to hand it over to God, and I had a peace in giving it to him. I didn't know what he was going to do, or even what his desire in this was, but he did, and that is what I rested in.

It was now almost four months after the accident. I knew for a couple weeks or so that one day soon, I would be served papers. I didn't know what to expect or what the papers would say. I was told by a couple of people that when the papers came, to just ignore what they said. They told me that it is just "legal mumbo jumbo." My friends were outside, very close to my van that night. They didn't even know Joy snuck out of the church; no one did. They knew what happened. I honestly thought each day that I didn't get served, that if it was going to come against me and hurt me, they'd let it go, that having a friend would mean more than what could be written.

Two days before the papers came, Greg and I had a long talk. He told me that they didn't want to have to go forward with a lawsuit, but since my insurance was fighting it, they had to. All I could say was okay. I didn't sleep well that night after our conversation. The next day when I woke up, I was a wreck thinking about it all. I was worried sick inside; I didn't know what to do or even what to think.

That morning, before I even sat down in my chair to read my Bible, God put this verse in my mind. "You will guard him and keep him in perfect peace whose mind is stayed on you, because he commits himself to you and leans on you and hopes confidently in you" (Isaiah 26:3 NIV). I was amazed at what God was telling me. He was promising me that if I kept my mind fixed on him, not what was going on around me; he would keep me in perfect peace.

Again, as I was stepping in the shower that same morning, he gave me this verse: "Fear not for I have redeemed you

I have called you by name, child you are mine. When you walk through the waters I will be there ... when you walk thru the fire, you will not be burned. For I am your God" (Isaiah 43:1–2 NIV). No matter what was ahead, God was promising me that he would walk with me, through all this. God flooded me with his peace at that moment, and I rested in him.

I didn't forget those verses, but the next day was different. No one could prepare me for what I read and how it would make me feel inside. I opened my mail that afternoon, and what I read crushed me. In order for them to win, their lawyer had to put total fault on me. It had to say that I was negligent and careless, that I was the cause of their child's death, and that I was the reason for their suffering.

I never felt so rejected and angry in my life, and I thought I was going to explode. I just cried. I couldn't sleep that night. I just lay there awake with my heart burning, asking God, "Now what do I do?" Over and over, all I could hear God whisper to me was, "Just step aside right now." So I did. Maybe my anger would have gotten in the way; I don't know.

Some people said to me, "That is just what they have to say to win; it's just insurance." Maybe that is the way the system works, maybe that is what they have to say to win, but my heart said this wasn't right. The only thing I wanted to hear was for my friends to tell me that what was written on those papers is not what they thought of me. That's all I wanted to hear. I left the church where we were serving together. I couldn't be there. If they would have told me they didn't agree with what was written against me, it would have changed everything, but they were silent. I didn't even want to talk to my friends right after I was served; it hurt so much. I really thought things would be settled and I would be back to church with them in just a couple weeks—or so I hoped.

It wasn't my money, but it was my name. A few people told me that it is a standard form letter, but to me it became personal when my name was written on it over and over. It hurt deeply, especially when it had to say I was the reason why they were all suffering. It hurt because that is where I faced my biggest battle each day; to have to fight those negative thoughts Satan would throw at my mind, and now it was on paper.

I knew God was still in control, but now I didn't have any idea what his plan was. Maybe this was part of his plan, I don't know. All I knew was that I was really hurting. I felt like my heart was on fire. I had talked to a pastor's wife and asked her what I should do. She could only say to me that she couldn't tell me what to do, but that I would really need to listen to God so he could direct me. So once again, he was the one that I poured out my heart and feelings to every day. As I cried out my hurts to him each day, he continued to soothe me with his peace, reminding me that he is in control.

I missed my church so much; I missed everyone. What was really hard was I never said goodbye to anyone. Week after week, all of the faces of the people I knew and the children that I taught and loved kept flooding my mind. It was so hard; I felt like I was abandoning everyone, but the rejection I felt inside was so strong that I couldn't even bear the thought to drive by the church. Every single day for months, I cried and asked God to let me go back to my church, to please restore the peace between my friends and me, to let this now be settled. Now I felt like he ripped a place I loved away from me too. Every time I would get on my knees and ask him, plead with him to let me go back, he would say to me over and over, "Be still and stay back."

Even though things weren't settled, I think I bugged God after a while. I did not like the uneasy feelings. It had been three months since I left, and I was still asking God to send me back, and his reply to me was, "It is not your concern if I send you back; your concern should be to pull even closer to me right now." So I finally quit bugging God. Instead I continued every day to get on my knees and surrender my desires to God, and I tucked in even closer to him.

Why would God ask me to step aside from a place I really loved? First, I have to give him my friends, now my church? I don't get it. Why wouldn't my friends just tell me that they didn't agree with what the papers said? Why were they so silent to me? I loved my friends. "God, why would you allow me to be the driver? This is such a horrible nightmare. I didn't ask for any of this. Why would you allow all this to happen? God, you know how much I love this family." I never in my life felt such a deep rejection. My heart broke.

I really wanted peace. After a few weeks, I tried calling them, writing them a letter, but there was only silence. I wanted to see my friends so badly during this time that we were separated so that we could all have peace. At first, I would look and hope I would run into them at the store or something, but then I heard God tell me one day to *stop looking and to just trust him*. So I surrendered my friends to God again, crying out on my knees day after day.

For a long time, every week, I had so many people calling and asking me to come back. I felt loved by everyone, but what made it hard was that the one who could let me return was God, and each time I asked him he said, "Not yet." I wanted so badly to obey God, but this was hard. I was a people pleaser, and I felt like I was letting all my friends down. But I knew God had told me to step aside and more than anything, I really wanted to obey God.

I did not know what God's plan was. I asked him to let them be blessed with it and give my friends favor with the insurance company. I didn't know what his will in this was. At times I felt so alone. But I wasn't. God was right there with me. God never let me down. He always reminded me that if I trusted him, he wouldn't fail me. I stayed strong in him and during this waiting time, developed a deeper level of trusting God. A trust that he knows what he is doing. I really wanted to see what he was going to do if I obeyed him and really trusted him.

As I was trusting God, I felt like I was walking with my eyes closed. Knowing what he was telling me to do and doing it, but not having any idea what was happening on the other end. There were many days that I wanted to give up and tell God, "That's it, I just want to go back. I can't stand the silence." Then I read in *The Battlefield of the Mind* book: "The devil will pound your mind to do something or to just give up too soon." I realized that he was the one trying to make me quit. He knows that if we give up too soon, we won't see the victory God has for us. So I just kept trusting. When God says wait, we need to wait because there is a reason.

Refuge

"God is my refuge. God is our refuge and strength, an ever-present help in time of trouble . . . "

Psalms 46:1 NIV

"He who dwells in the shelter of the most High, will rest in the shadow of the Almighty. I will say of the Lord, He is my refuge and my fortress, my God in whom I will trust."

Psalms 91:1–2 NIV

A few days before I left the church where the accident happened, I heard a sermon on the radio that morning. It talked about how, back in the Old Testament days, God sent people to a place of refuge. In Exodus 21:12–13 NIV it says, "If a person causes an accident and someone dies and it wasn't intentional, but God lets it happen. He is to go to a place of refuge until things are settled." I was surprised that I heard this. I thought about that and tucked it away in my heart that morning. That afternoon, I was served the papers.

The rejection I felt from my friends after I was served papers was too much for me. I left my church and went back to the church I grew up in. I know that God asked me to step aside. Even though I really missed my church, I would walk through the doors of where God led me back to. I didn't even need to see or talk to anyone because I could feel God's arms wrap around me. His peace just flooded me. I was so amazed by this. How could that be, not even needing to speak to anyone? Just being inside the church, I could feel his presence just begin to rush over me and start healing me, week after week. The peace was amazing. It was so soothing.

The first Sunday I was there, twice during the service, two older women who didn't know why I came back to that church came up to me, each at different times. I didn't tell either of them what I was carrying inside. But each one looked at me, hugged me, and said to me with confidence, "No weapon formed against you shall prosper" (Isaiah 54:17 NIV). It was as if God was reminding me that he was walking with me through all this and he would protect me from any attack the enemy would try to throw at me. No one ever asked me why I came back to that church; they just hugged me and loved me. I still really bugged God during the week to let me go back to the other church, but each time I went to where he led me, his peace was so amazingly strong.

God is our refuge. He knows what we need. He does know what we can bear, and he will not give us any more that we can handle. As time passed, he finally told me one of the reasons he had me step aside was to heal me. Even though people loved me at the church where the accident happened, it was very hard to go there each week. I battled with it inside of me each week I was there. I desperately wanted to be there for my friends more than words can describe. I wanted to walk with them through this. My heart just bled for them. Each week, I would leave the church where the accident happened and cry, even though I could not have prevented the accident. It was hard to be freed from the guilt I still carried when I saw their loss.

God brought me to a place of peace, a place to worship him, and a place to be taught without my mind going in other directions because of the accident. I realized that staying where I was; I couldn't heal fully in my mind. I would constantly be wondering every time I saw my friends, what they were thinking of me. He had to move me. I was in awe when I realized one day, that even though it was one of the hardest, most painful moves for me, he loved me enough to do what is really best for me. God will give you peace as you follow his lead.

Forgiving

After the accident, I ran to God. He was my comfort, my strength. A hunger to know him deeper just flooded me. Reading God's Word and other Christian books spoke truth to me. I would spend a lot of time reading each day. Reading became very healing to me. A few weeks after I was served the papers, I was shopping, and I told God while I was at the store that I needed a new book to read. Nothing stood out to me so I decided to wait. The next day a friend came over to have lunch with me. While we were visiting, she said she had something for me—a book. She told me that it was really on her heart to give me this. I'd have to say that the title of the book was humbling to receive, but I just asked God for a book and here he put it on her heart to give it to me. The book was *Total Forgiveness* by R.T. Kendall.

Ouch! I had asked God to show me if there was anything in me that he didn't want in my heart, but this was humbling. I decided to read it. I realized that I somehow had anger and bitterness in my heart and I needed to learn how to totally forgive. If I was going to walk in love and be free, I needed to forgive totally.

Greg and Sara were in such a deep pain with the loss of their daughter, maybe they didn't know that I was hurting. But no matter what, I still had to deal with this issue in my heart. I learned the one who gains the most from forgiving is not the one you're forgiving but you. You may not think you have unforgiveness and bitterness in your heart, but if you look closely at yourself, you may notice that inner peace isn't there like it was before. The only thing that will bring back that peace to you is you forgiving and letting go of whatever you're holding onto, even if it was something a very long time ago.

Only God and you know what is in your heart, and if it stays there and grows, then you're only hurting yourself. Even if you can't totally forget, you shouldn't dwell on it. It will only hurt you. I found out that you need to do it over and over because bitterness can easily seep back in. Someone or something can remind you of what someone did to you, or the enemy may try to whisper to you and bring up how hurt you were about whatever you went through, even years later. Bitterness can easily sneak back in and if it does, you need to lay it down and forgive again in your heart so you can be free.

Even if they could never tell me that what the papers I was served with said about me wasn't how they felt about me, I still needed to forgive and let it go. Even if you never have the chance to talk to that person again, inside you will have victory and be free. When you can truly and totally forgive, it is amazing because it goes against your flesh. It can be equal to a miracle. God paid a huge price for us to be forgiven. It is the greatest thing he has done, sending his Son to die on the cross for our sins so we can be free. "God has forgiven us and we need to forgive others" (Colossians 3:13 NIV).

God's Hand

God whispered to me, "Your faith in me allows me to be faithful to you."

One day God asked me an interesting question. As I was reading the Bible that day, I felt God asking me, "Do you understand how powerful I am? Do you understand that at any moment everything can change at my command?"

I was humbled that he would ask me that, and I said to him, "Yes, I do, but why would you ask me that?" I thought about that question and thought, *Maybe I don't really know how powerful you are.* I told God, "I know you wouldn't be asking me that question if I really knew." So now I was on a search to see how powerful God really is.

Night after night, I got out my Bible to search out how powerful God is. I was amazed beyond words at how powerful he is. There are so many verses that talk about how powerful God is. He is God; he can do anything. Isaiah 44:24 NIV says, "This is what the LORD says, your Redeemer, who formed you in the womb. I am the LORD who has made all things, who alone stretched out the heavens, who spread out the earth by Myself."

How awesome our God is; he alone has created everything! There is no one like God. Also Isaiah 41:10 NIV says, "Do not fear for I am with you; do not be dismayed for I am your God. I will strengthen you and help you. I will uphold you with my righteous right hand." God promises to be with us in that verse, to strengthen us and help us, and he promises to keep you in his hand. Everything is in his hands. What a powerful God!

My mind was still being hit with thoughts about the accident and now I really battled feeling rejected. Every day there was such a heaviness on my heart. The only way I could get it to lift off me was to go before God and surrender my heartaches and thoughts to him. Day after day, God carried it; he comforted me and promised me he would protect me and that he would never let me down. I hung onto that. Every day I kept reminding God of his promises. One of my favorite promises is Isaiah 49:23 NIV: "Those who hope in you will not be disappointed." I would remind God that he said if I put my hope and trust in him, that he promised he would not disappoint me, so I strongly held him to that.

I remember driving one day, consumed and stressed inside, thinking about what would happen when the deposition and court dates came. I was filled with so much anxiety that I just cried. I wondered what would be said. Would their lawyer be nice? And God reminded me, "Did I not tell you I'd be with you? Why are you worrying?"

I forgot. I needed to remember what God spoke to my heart. I told God, "If you allowed all this to happen, then I do expect you to be with me. I expect you to be by my side." There was a great peace that came with knowing he is right by my side, all the time.

God became so real to me during this time. He has been there. We forget that Jesus has been right where we are. You may think, *But he hasn't had to go through what I have*. But he has. He has felt every feeling we have felt, but even greater. He has felt rejection, sorrow, loneliness, pain, grief, anger, joy, love, and so on. He has been there, and he became my greatest comfort. To know that my creator has felt the feelings that I have and understood those feeling amazed me. I know we learn about that in church, but it wasn't until I was brought to this place, that I began to fully comprehend this better. I felt such a closeness with God, to just know that he has felt it all, that he has been there. I am not alone. I still sit and think about it all, and it puts me in awe of God.

It had been almost five months from the time I left my church. I had only spoken to my friends once during that time. It was a Monday, a couple days before the three of us were to give our deposition of the accident. My heart felt so heavy, like a brick was placed on my chest. As I was driving that afternoon, I just cried, not understanding why we were all going through this. I had had enough. I didn't want to keep enduring the memories of the accident. Everything inside me wanted to scream. I loved Joy and my friends. I wanted it to end and be back to normal. I wanted this nightmare to be erased and for Joy to be here again. She was supposed to be here! This wasn't supposed to happen! Make it stop! As I was driving, God whispered to me, "Just hang on, hang on." So I listened and hung on, not knowing at all what he was up to, but if he was telling me to hang on, I would hang on.

Tuesday morning everything was confirmed for the next day. That afternoon I got a call from my pastor, and he asked how I was. I told him that there was a heaviness on my heart. Well, he told me that my friends wanted him to call me and let me know that they just dropped the entire lawsuit. He said they just realized it became personal and they didn't want to hurt me.

I expected to walk with God through the whole ordeal. I didn't expect him to let everything drop the day before the deposition. God's timing is what really surprised me.

I didn't ask them to drop it. All I wanted to hear was that what was written wasn't what they thought of me. It was one of the biggest things I have seen God do in my life. He was so faithful. I thanked God that he didn't answer my prayer right away after I was served the papers, even though walking through that time was so painful. Now, looking back at how I learned to really trust God during that time, I realize how much I have grown. I couldn't have learned to really trust God and watch him be faithful if I didn't have to wait on him. I needed to learn to just wait on him and trust that he knew what he was doing. To know that he knew what he was doing, even though it really hurt me, was worth totally trusting him and seeing him be faithful.

I was thinking about God one day, and I asked him why he is so good and faithful. He said, "Because you believed and trusted me. Your faith in me allows me to be faithful to you. I will show you my power as you trust me."

What are you facing today that you need to trust God

to do something? Do you need to be healed or to find a job? Are you worried about your finances? Do you need to be set free from something? I cannot tell you how your circumstance will turn out. But I can tell you that as you put your hope and trust in God, follow what he asks of you. He will be faithful to you. It may not always be the answer you're looking for or turn out the way you want it to, but if you will truly believe, he can come through for you in the very best way—his way.

You need to patiently wait on his timing and, during that time, get in the Bible and get to know God in a better way. Find his promises, stand on them, and truly believe them. What keeps us from seeing God's hand move is a lack of faith. You need to believe that God is true to his Word. You need to believe that he can do anything, and then obey what he asks of you.

I remember getting so mad at God for allowing all this to happen. I was so mad, I thought, *What did I do to deserve to be the one that was the driver?* I truly cared and loved my friends. I loved Joy so much. To have to carry the burden for Joy's death and to know how painful it is for my friends, to be aching for their daughter, just tore me up inside.

As God began to work in my life, he began to reveal himself to me in such amazing ways. I developed a closeness with him and began to find Jesus as my comforter, my best friend. I was able to find a place of stillness to hear him and truly love him with my whole heart. I asked him again in love, "God, what did I do to deserve this, to know you the way I do."

I wouldn't trade knowing God the way I do for anything.

I was humbled and told God, "Who am I to truly know you to the depth you've revealed yourself to me?" I was in awe that he brought me to this intimate relationship with him, a relationship that is worth far more than anything.

God can take something that was so horrible and use it for his glory. You have to be willing to put all trust and belief in him, because that will change everything. You have to be willing to look to him, and him alone, to fill that void or heartache. You need to be willing to release it to him. It will take time, but he will not fail you, he will be faithful.

Now What?

And God reminded me... *my peace will always guide you.*

It was now seven months since we left the church we were at, almost a year after the accident. My friends and I had talked a little, and it was healing. Greg really wanted us to come back to church. This is what I had been waiting for.

I was ready; this was it. I asked God over and over for weeks what I should do. Should I go back? The only thing I could hear God tell me was, "I will bless whatever decision you make on this." That wasn't the answer I wanted; I just wanted him to tell me where to go. I had been listening to him tell me to wait all these months, and now he left this decision up to me. *God, don't let me decide.*

I prayed, thought about it, and my decision was to go back to the church where the accident happened. I told many people I was going back. I was determined and excited; this was what I had been waiting for.

We went one Sunday. I was nervous but at the same time excited. But as I was walking into the church that morning, the enemy pounded my mind with thoughts like, "People are going to think you're such a loser for leaving," etc. I wanted to run. I realized God wouldn't tell me that. I refused to listen to the enemy's lies, because I knew it was God that asked me to step aside, even if others didn't understand.

Everyone was nice and really glad to see us. I felt so loved. But my heart just ached as I was there. I kept thinking about the accident. Everything around me reminded me of Joy and my friends. As I sat in the service, I had such a heaviness; all I could think was, *God, I don't want to be here.*

I went home sad and asked God, "What was that? What do I do? This is what I wanted so badly, and now I don't want it? I have a lot of heartache here. The church you sent me to heal in was so full of peace for me. Why would I leave that peace? Now what? God, this is what I have begged you for all these months, and now I don't know if I want it. I don't get it."

I had so many people sharing their thoughts with me about what I should do. I was such a huge wreck for weeks, trying to figure out where I should go. I didn't expect my heart to change. Greg really wanted us there, but we had not worked on our friendship at all. How awkward that would be? They really wanted us back at church with them, but I was told that, for now, the friendship would have to move really slowly. I missed my friends so much that I just ached to be close to them. That is what I wanted more than being at church with them. I really wanted my friendship restored, but I needed that friendship first to mend and start to grow again outside of the church. During the next couple of months after our visit back to the church, I tried calling them a few times to talk to them. I left messages for them, but there was no response back.

I kept seeking God in what to do and where to go. Finally, God reminded me of something—that his peace would always guide me. I would know what to do because I had peace from God. I didn't go back. I stayed where I had great peace.

God really has a sense of humor. I didn't expect that to happen! I bugged him so much to let me go there and when it came down to finally having what I wanted, it wasn't what I really wanted anymore. A friend told me that it was probably what God wanted me to see. It's true; I would have never known where I was to go if I didn't go back. I would've always wondered. I needed God to show me that. Nothing can compare to the peace God can give us.

God's Love

"Nothing can separate us from God's love, nothing . . . "
Romans 8:38–39 NIV

God's love for us is amazing. I loved God my whole life, I really did. I knew he loved me, but it wasn't until being in my darkest moments did I really grasp how much he loves us. I remember feeling so low right after the accident, a day where I really wanted to just die. I felt like a failure and the guilt was taking over me when God said to me one day, "My love for you has not changed. You need to remember who you are in me; you are my child."

His love for me hasn't changed? When he spoke that to my heart, it just amazed me. Somehow, even though I knew what happened was totally an accident, I still thought less of myself. For God to remind me that no matter what I have done or what happens in my life, his love for me never changes, made me want to look to him even more.

It doesn't matter what you've done or where you've been; God loves you the same. You cannot earn God's love; it's always there. It's free, and he is just waiting for you to believe him and grab hold of his love. "Nothing can separate us from Gods love, nothing…" (Romans 8:38–39 NIV).

Every single day for three months, I would cry out and ask, "God, do my friends know how much I really love them? I feel like they don't because look what happened… God I love them so much, will they remember that?" After the accident, I was consumed with these questions.

One day as I was spending time with God, he asked me something that surprised me. He said to me, "Let's talk about that question you keep asking me."

I said, "What?"

He said to me, "Do you know how much I love you? Do you know how deeply I feel for you? I truly love you. I cry. I long for you to know and remember what I've done for you. I gave my life. I long for you to know my heart and see my love. I ask you, do you, will you remember and grasp how much I love you and want you? I gave everything so I could have you with me. I created you because I wanted you. I wanted you. I ask you the same, do you know, really know how much I love you? Do you? Please don't forget it. Think on me and remember my love for you."

Every time I think about what God spoke to my heart I just want to cry. I didn't expect God to answer me that way. I was waiting for him to tell me, "Yes, they know you love them." But instead, he told me of his love, his love that is so deep. He wanted me to know the depth of love he has for us. The understanding that I was created just because God wanted me caused me to love him even more. The times I would cry and ask God that question, my heart just ached to know the answer. So when God asked me that question back, I can only believe that his heart aches with such a passionate love for us that we don't really grasp the depth of his love and he longs for us to know.

God knew what I really needed to hear. I didn't need to keep asking him that question anymore because I had his love. I knew that he knew what was in my heart and that was all that mattered. God wants us to know how much he loves us. If we could grasp it, we'd be different. I believe we'd act and do things differently. We'd want to please him so much.

In the first three months after the accident, I bugged God with that question: "Do my friends know how much I love them?" About fourteen months after the accident, I received an e—mail from Sara thanking me for loving them like family and how much that meant to them. I just cried. Then, I received a phone call from Greg. That was the first time they called in over a year. I was in shock for days. It was wonderful. Greg talked about our friendship and the depth and love that was there. I was in awe.

When God first answered my question, he showed me his love. Over a year later, he showed me that they remembered how much I cared for and loved them. God knew exactly what I needed to know first. I needed to grasp God's love first to pull me through the hardest year of my life. I needed to know how much he loved me so I could really trust him to walk with me and teach me his ways. It's easier to trust someone that really loves you. I wanted to obey God even more because of his love.

Something happened to me after he showed me his love. When I was shopping or out walking, I began to look at people and my heart would just ache. I'd look at them, and in my mind, I'd ask God, "Do they know how much you love them? Do they know that you created them just because you wanted them?" People need to know. God wants others to know how much he truly loves us. Will you show them? What are you going through that feels too heavy to carry? God is there to carry it for you. He is there to pour out his love on you, heal you, and mend you. He wants you to know that, no matter what you're going through, his love for you never changes. He knows what is best for you. You may be doubting that and thinking, *If he knew what was best, I wouldn't be having to walk through this hard time.* I know I think that a lot. But what he wants you to know is that he is always by your side. In Hebrew 13:5 NIV he promises that he will never leave us and he will never forsake us. He will help you make it through the hardest thing that you're facing. God understands how you feel, and no matter what, he loves you to a depth that is so deep. His love is meant to carry us through our hardest times. He loves us so much.

One day, I was hanging out with God, talking to him and I said, "LORD, I unload to you each day what's heavy on my heart and you fill me with your promises, but today, I want to know what is on your heart. What are you thinking about today?" I didn't have a clue what he'd say to me; I just wanted to know. As I sat before him and before I even finished my question, he said to me, "Souls, I think about souls. My heart deeply aches for them." I was in awe! I didn't expect him to say that. As I thought about what he said, it just brought tears to my eyes and my heart just ached. He is thinking so much about the lost and how he loves them so deeply. As much as we greatly desire something, God greatly desires souls. He wants us to reach them, to be his hands, to show them Jesus. He loves us so much that he doesn't want any to perish, for that is why he came to save us. Romans 5:8 NIV says, "He demonstrated his love for us, He laid down his life for us, even while we were still sinners so we could be saved." He loves us so much that he gave everything so we could be with him forever.

God cares about the littlest details, more than we do. He knows your needs. After the accident, I hadn't thought much of my van, other than I was never going to drive it again. We put it in the garage until we could get rid of it. I didn't have the energy to even try to think about something different to drive. My pastor talked to me one day and asked me what I was going to do with my van. I told him I was going to sell it. He said that God put it on a couple's heart to give their van to us. I said, "Absolutely not... *no*! This is way too big... I will feel indebted to them... no!" I have a hard time with receiving. I'd rather give to others than have to receive. But he said we didn't have a choice because God put it on their heart.

The couple brought the van over to our house and gave it to us. It was only four years old with about 50,000 miles on it; it was just beautiful. The van was humbling to receive; I did not want to accept it. The couple was so excited to do what God placed on their hearts. It was as if they were the ones receiving something. The funny thing was they weren't. They were giving us something. We received it, and you know, it was well above anything we could afford or even think to buy. I cried and sat in awe of God and thought, *God, you would do this for us?*

My husband and I looked at the color, and we said, "God is funny; he even gave it to us with the very detail of the color we always wanted. God is good, so good. Even with the van, I felt his love. He didn't need to do that for us, I was just in awe that he would.

God shows us his love through people. I can't get out of my mind the day of the funeral. I was really crying, and I looked up and saw my oldest brother kneeling before me. I looked at him, and he looked at me and he wiped away my tears with his hand and then he held me. To me it was like Jesus was kneeling before me, looking into my eyes, and wiping away my tears, wrapping his arms around me. As much as your heart aches for someone when they are going through a hard time and you desire to hold them up, it is nothing compared to how much God desires to hold you up. God wants to hold you and pour out his love on you at least a thousand times more. He desperately wants to carry you through; let him. We are to love others and show God's love to them. It is God's desire for us to see his love.

Focus

> *"One thing I do, forgetting what is behind and straining toward what is ahead."*
>
> *Philippians 3:13* NIV

How do you keep going when everything around you is a mess? How do you keep going when in a split second everything changes to a nightmare? No matter what it is that you're going through, you need to learn how to stay focused. How do you do that when you feel like there is no hope, when you can't see past the mess you're in? So many days I would cry and feel so depressed. I would tell God, "I just want to go home, please take me to heaven. I am done. I don't want to think about this anymore. I can't bear the memory of it all. Please take me away from it all."

People would look at me and say, "You know it was totally an accident," but they weren't battling the thoughts in my mind. How could I keep going and bearing what was so heavy on my heart? Joy and her family meant so much to me. Why would God allow this to happen with my friends that meant so much to me? That did not make any sense to me. No one could help me just forget it all. The littlest thing would remind me of it all or of my friends.

It must have been a couple months after the accident when I was still consumed with carrying the load of the accident. I felt God whisper to me, "Don't look back" (Philippians 3:13 NIV). Don't look back? How do you do that? How can you not look behind you? It is hard. I was not going to forget Joy or my friends, but I realized I had to stop looking back at the accident if I was going to get stronger. It wasn't easy to not look back at everything. It was something God would have to remind me of continually, and it was work. But something happened when I tried my hardest to not look back.

That is where my focus started. I had to try my hardest to not look back at yesterdays and try to look at only today. I began living for today, the day God gave me. We are only guaranteed today. Yesterday is gone, and I cannot possibly do anything to change what happened. Tomorrow isn't here, so why should I worry about a day that's not even here yet. I needed to learn how to live just for today. It made me look at life differently. A lot of stress was lifted when I was just taking one day at a time.

To not look back is not easy. I had to get down on my knees and surrender daily the things that weighed on me, everything that was behind me. I had to continually let it go and hand it to God over and over. I had to choose that, no matter what was going on all around me, I would still glorify God.

I remember when I was really missing my church, God would tell me again not to look back. That was really hard. I cried so much. I really loved it there and I loved the people.

Behind me were a lot of good memories and people I loved. But If I was to be of any use to God where he's placed me now, I had to give it back to God every single day and not look behind me, even if what was behind me was good.

A friend shared this verse with me one day: "No one who puts his hand to the plow and looks back is fit for the service in the kingdom of God" (Luke 9:62 NIV). God still wants to use us, and if our focus is on yesterday or behind us, we can't be used the way he wants to use us today. Picture a bird flying. A bird can't fly straight and get to where it wants to be if it is looking back behind itself. It would stumble and bump into things, and it would be really slowed down. Looking back distracts your vision for today.

I realized life on earth is temporary and that these feeling wouldn't be something that I was going to have to carry with me forever. I would tell God, "I know you can help me make it through all this. And someday, when I am with you, there will be no more tears, no more pain." I focused on eternity.

God has a purpose for each one of us. Since I was going to go day by day, every morning I would wake up and tell God that I wanted to fulfill that purpose for just today, whatever it may be. One day I asked God, "What if I didn't do anything today or make a difference or talk to anyone, what would the purpose for today be?"

He said, "Just drawing closer to me today would have been the purpose." God wants that closeness with us. He wants us to be intimate with him. He wants our focus to be on him.

Our thoughts can get us in trouble. You need to try your hardest to focus on God's thoughts that are written in the

Bible. The more time you spend with him and in the Word, the more you'll receive from it, and the stronger you will become. You may think, *It won't matter if I just skip spending a little time with him today; I'll be fine.* But so easily that one day can turn into many days, because we get so distracted and busy, even serving him.

One day God showed me how to picture it this way: As you know God and spend time with him, you are covered in his armor, his protection. But each day that we don't look to him and seek him, it's like a tiny pinhole pokes through that armor. It doesn't seem like it would do anything. But day after day, pinhole after pinhole, all of a sudden there's an opening. You're a little weaker, and it opens you up to be hit easier by the enemy. You need to look to God each day, even if it is for five minutes so you can stay strong and ready.

To stay focused, you need to remind yourself daily of what God has for you. He has a plan and a purpose for your life that is not yet fulfilled. He created you for a reason. You need to stay focused on God to make it. I can so easily go back to the night of the accident and everything that followed it, and be very depressed. There are days, I admit, that I forget to stay focused. I start to feel depressed, I start to feel like Joy is gone because of me, and that is very hard to pull out of. It can come in and hit me out of nowhere, when I least expect it, and cause me to cry. It starts to hurt inside all over again. So easily at that moment, I want to give up and wish I didn't have to keep going. When that happens, I have to try my hardest to remember what the Bible says. I have to remember the promises God has given us in his Word. I start to say them, and you know as I start reminding God of his promises and I worship him, my focus becomes clearer again and the heaviness that was on me begins to lift.

You need to try your hardest to remember that God is in control, he knows the future. He will make all this work out for good in his way and his timing. You need to focus on making it just one day at a time. Look to God; focus on him and his will for you. What you're facing is so temporary compared to eternity … focus on eternity.

Set Free

It was my choice whether I wanted to be free…

How was I going to be able to walk along side my friends, week after week, grieving, and not think about how they would not be hurting if I had not been driving my van that night? How could I ever be free to not carry this load? How could my thoughts be freed from this? It was about six weeks after the accident, and I cried out to God and told him that I desperately needed him to help me. I needed to see myself as everyone else saw me and as he saw me.

God showed me that it was my choice whether I wanted to be set free from the driver's seat. I had to be willing to let it go and let God set me free. I had to be willing to surrender the accident to him. I could easily hang onto it or, even after God set me free, pick it back up again. I needed to listen to God, to his truth, and believe I could be free.

I wanted to be free, but I had to get myself out of the driver's seat. When I saw myself as God saw me, as his child, and realized that no matter what, his love for us does not change, I started to feel freedom. I had to refuse to let the lies of the enemy pound me by continually getting on my knees to worship God daily. To be free you need to stay focused. Focus on God and what he has for you, not dwelling on what happened. Stay focused on God's promises and what the Bible says, even though what has happened is not fair. If you allow God to speak to your heart and you release the burden to him, he will use it for his good. I need you to know that it may take many, many times of releasing it to him over and over, but you need to continually release it to him in order to stay free.

It is a battle to stay free, because the enemy easily throws back in your face what has happened. Satan wants to distract you any way he can to get your focus off God and his plan for your life. God wants us to be free. You need to listen to the truth. Make a choice to continually let go of what happened and give it to God. He wants us to release it to him so we can heal.

It is your choice, as it was mine, to release it to him. Don't be bound by the past.

I know that I know that it was an accident and there was nothing I could've done to prevent it, but I still carried it. There are still days, from time to time, that I think about Joy and I just want to scream, and I think if only I hadn't driven up to say goodbye, or if I would've stayed longer it wouldn't have happened. In those moments, it feels very heavy. In those moments, I don't feel free. I start to carry it all over again, and I feel as if I am sinking. But it is then God reminds me to give what weighs heavy on my heart to him again.

God wants you to be free. Are you ready for him to set you free? "Him who the Son sets free is free indeed" (John 8:36 NIV). That is a promise. Grab hold of it. Jesus paid the price for you to be free. No matter what you're facing, Jesus will bring you freedom.

Satan wants you to stay bound and depressed. But "Jesus came to give life and life more abundantly" (John 10:10 NIV). How many times has the past wrecked today? It has happened to me too many times. Don't let the past rob you of today and what God has for you. You cannot do yesterday again. Today is a fresh new day, a day that you only get once. Don't let Satan take that away from you. Let go of what you're carrying, no matter how heavy it is, and surrender it to Jesus so you can be free. He will bring your joy back; he will give you hope, for he promised in *Jeremiah 29:11* NIV, *He knows the plans he has for you, for peace and not harm, to give you a future and a hope.*

Jesus created you for a purpose. Your purpose isn't fulfilled yet. Jesus has so much more for you. Let him set you free. Hand whatever you're carrying to him. To be free you have to let go of it. When the enemy tries to bind you, remember you are free and refuse to listen to the lies of the enemy. He will give up when he knows you won't give in. Stand firm.

Even as I write this book, it's hard. God has set me free, but as I look back to tell you what he's done in my life, Satan has tried over and over to throw the accident in my face. He tries to hit my mind and make me depressed. But that's where the fight is; am I going to fall for that and be bound or will I fight to stay free? I will fight. I will worship, I will tuck in close to God with everything in me, and I will cause the enemy to flee. You need to fight.

God's heart aches so much for you to be free from whatever you're facing in your life. He doesn't want you to live bound by what's happened. He came so we could be free. Lay it down at his feet. When you allow God to set you free, you will feel freedom again. You will feel joy; you will feel peace. Let him restore you to whom he created you to be.

You may be reading my book and not know God the way I do. You may think to yourself, *I don't know a God like that.* God wants to be your best friend; he wants to fill you with his truths. He wants you to know him in such an intimate way. You may be walking through the most difficult, painful time of your life and feel so alone. I felt so alone, but I wasn't. This same God who carried me through this is there to carry you too. He wants to help you, but he can't unless you accept him in your heart. Give him your heart. Jesus came so we could be saved, so we could be free. He gave his life for us so we could be forgiven and live with him in heaven forever.

If you don't know Jesus in a personal way, then I ask you right now as you're reading this to look to the one who created you. We don't know what the future holds, we're not even promised tomorrow, and we only have today. God is very real. He is right beside you, right now, tugging at your heart. He loves you to a depth that is so very deep, and no matter what, his love for you does not change. Look to Jesus. He created you because he wanted you; he's given you the very breath you breathe right now.

No one is perfect; "all have sinned and fallen short of the glory of God" (Romans 3:23). If you want to know Jesus in a personal way ask him to come into your heart. "Confess your sins and he will forgive you and you will be free" (1 John 1:9 NIV). Give your life to Jesus and let him be LORD over your life. The only way to spend eternity with God is by asking him to come into your heart, asking for forgiveness, and living for him. In this life, you will still go through hard times, but with Jesus inside you, those hard times will be more peaceful because Jesus is walking through it with you. He is our hope and our peace. He will never fail you. I promise you, you will not be disappointed. Let Jesus walk with you through your life. Let him set you free.

Restore

"And the God of all grace, who called you to his eternal glory in Christ, after you have suffered a little while, will himself restore you and make you strong, firm, and steadfast."

1 Peter 5:10 NIV

God asked me to do things that, for me, were big sacrifices, and at times it did not make any sense. But God knew what was best for me. One day, God reminded me that in bible days, when he wanted to do something great, his ways did not always make sense. But when his people still obeyed, he showed himself faithful and true in a great way.

I will be honest and tell you that, when he asked me to let go of my friends during this time, I really questioned him. I obeyed, but at times, it hurt so deeply to follow his lead. Still some days, I question him on why, but then some days, I realized that he has been healing my heart and mind. I know that is what was truly important for him to do in my life. I could have chosen not to follow his lead and had what I wanted, but then my healing would have been slower. We think we know what is the best thing for us, but God really knows what is best. He loves you enough to do what is best for you.

When you give God what you're carrying, it no longer becomes your burden, but God's. I believe when we reach for him with all we have, we will find him; he will fill us with himself. When you desire God more than anything, he will show himself to you in amazing ways.

God wants to restore you. He wants you to hope again and to live again. I cannot tell you how your journey will turn out. I don't even know at this point how my story will end. But no matter how it turns out, I am sure of this one thing: If you stay close to Jesus and let him walk with you through what you're facing, he will bring joy, peace, and freedom back to you. He will set you free.

You can live without carrying the heavy load; it just takes time and the willingness to surrender it to God. I have to surrender the accident still to this day; if I don't, I will be consumed with the load of everything. The weight and anxiety will fill me. In those moments, my vision is not clear, but clouded. Trust him, even if you have to surrender your heartache to him everyday for the rest of your life. Each time you hand your worries to him, he will pour his fresh peace over you. As you continue to hand your cares to God, the load you carry will get lighter.

God wants to restore you; he wants to use you. He can use a surrendered heart better than one that tries to hang on to the situation. Give your heartache to Jesus so that you can be free. Let him be your very closest friend, and let Him fill that void. God will restore you. He will not leave you in sadness forever, because he promised in 1 Peter 5:10 NIV,

"... he will himself restore you and make you strong, firm and steadfast." That is a promise. Hang onto that and expect him to restore you. Then let him!

You need to go one day at a time. We are not guaranteed tomorrow, so focus on making the most of today. Tomorrow, when you wake up in the morning, focus again on making it through just that day. Something happens when you do that; life seems to go better, because you're not trying to figure out the rest of your life, just that day. God wants all of you. If you can look to him and know that he is in control and follow him, you will have joy. Life may be different than what you have planned, but different can be good if God is in control. "For those who hope in you will not be disappointed ..." (Isaiah 49:23 NIV). Put your hope in him!

I do still think about Greg and Sara every day and I really love them. I think about how much they must miss Joy. I think about them and I pray so much that God would continue to fill them with his peace. My heart and arms ache for them, to hold and comfort them. Many days I still want things to be back to the way they were and I cry, I argue with God. But during those moments when I feel like that, God continues to gently remind me that my weakness will be my strength. I find that is true on those days when I feel so weak, when the memory of the accident overwhelms me, and I just want to run away from it all. Even more, that is when I need to run to God, so he can strengthen me again, so he can fill me fresh with his hope and peace, and so he can teach me more of who he is.

He will use your weakness, it will become your strength, and it will bring forth beauty that can only come from going through the hard places you have walked through. Isaiah 45:3 NIV, "I will give you treasures of darkness, riches stored in secret places, so that you may know that I am the LORD God who summons you by name." One thing God desires greatly is that we know him in an intimate way. He wants to be our closest friend, our comforter, our everything. I believe, as this verse says, that God gives us these treasures of darkness, times of walking through hard times, to bring us to a place to truly know him. I walked with God my whole life. I knew him. I loved him. But walking through this most painful experience, right in the thick of it all, brought me to a place to really know God in such a real way. I wanted to feel his heart. I wanted for him to share his joys and his heartaches with me. I longed for that intimacy. To *know* him through all you go through is the treasure. To *know* him in a deeper, intimate way is riches stored in secret places. I don't know if I would have slowed down enough in life to know him to the depth I do now.

As I sit here and think about where God has brought me to in my life today, the people he has surrounded me with, how I am serving him, I think back to that quote that I was determined to believe: "What God desires for our lives will bring true happiness, give us the most peace and joy. God's desires will satisfy our souls deeply. We just need to trust him and be satisfied in God alone."

I was determined. I really wanted to know what God's desires were for my life. I wanted to be truly satisfied in God alone and his plan for me. I knew what I wanted, I knew what I thought would make me so happy. I thought what would make me the happiest would be for everything to go back to the way it was before the accident. Many, many days I questioned God on his direction.

It took me over a year and a half to see the fruit of following his steps, and not hanging on to what I wanted. It has given me a great peace and joy that nothing else can compare to. It has brought me to a deeper love for Jesus in my life. There is a peace that only God can give; he can be trusted. It is totally worth taking that step of faith to hear him and follow him, because his ways are much better than our ways.

As I laid down my desires in exchange for his, he became the one I desired more than anything. He took the places in my heart that were broken, and he filled those places with him. I now know what God's desire for me was. As I was out for a walk one day God said to me, "Do you want to know what my desire for you is?"

I said, "Yes, I do."

And God said to me, "My ultimate desire for you is for you to know me in such an intimate way, and to truly love me. For in that you will have the most peace and joy." I cried when he spoke that to my heart because it is true. God is what brings me the most joy and peace more than anything else in this world could. Nothing can compare to him. God really will give you the most peace and joy. Trust him.

What God has ahead for you will be greater than what was behind, if you look to him. It cannot get better if you don't hand him the circumstances. Starting now, let this day be better than the past. Continue daily to let go and give what you're carrying to God. He will not let you down; trust him. God wants to restore you; he wants you to hope again. He has created you for a purpose, but more than anything, he wants you to love him with everything, for in that you will find freedom, peace, and joy.

Epilogue

It's been three years from the date of the accident. My friendship with Greg and Sara has had small steps of healing. We have had a few times of spending time together, and the friendship is slowly healing. They now live in a different state. I still think about them each day and pray for God's peace on them. I believe God will be faithful to continue to bring a greater healing in our friendship in the future. Greg and Sara, I love you!

Notes

Introduction:

Joshua 24:15

Worship:

Zephaniah 3:17 (KJV)

Psalms 22:3 (KJV)

2 Corinthians 12:9

2 Corinthians 12:12

Psalms 28:7

Psalms 55:12

Philippians 4:7

Best friend:

Proverbs 18:24

John 14

Isaiah 9:6

Psalms 62:8

Psalms 139:1

Hebrews 6:10

Obedience:

Why, by Ann Gram Lotz

Purpose-driven Life, by Rick Warren

John 14:15

Deuteronomy 6:5

Deuteronomy 13:3

John 14:15

Patience and Trust:

Battlefield of the Mind, by Joyce Meyers

Proverbs 3:4–5

Hebrews 13:8

James 1:3

Philippians 1:6

Jeremiah 29:11

Isaiah 49:23

Psalms 91:14

Isaiah 48:18–19

Hebrews 13:5

Giving It to God:

Psalms 25:1–2

Isaiah 26:3

Isaiah 43:1–2

Refuge:

Psalms 91:1–2

Exodus 21:12–13

Isaiah 54:17

Forgive:

Col 3:13

God's Love:

Romans 8:38–39

Hebrews 13:5

Romans 5:8

Focus:

Philippians 3:13

Luke 9:62

Set Free:

John 8:38

John 10:10

Jeremiah 29:11

Romans 3:23

1 John 1:9

Restore:

1 Peter 5:10

Isaiah 29:23

Isaiah 45:3